Purposeful Prayers

*31 Prayers to Encourage and Empower You
to Stay Connected and Committed to God's
Will & Way*

Purposeful Prayers: 31 Prayers to Encourage and Empower You to Stay Connected and Committed to God's Will & Way

Other Titles by Author

Renew: 40 Prayers and Prompts to Power Up Your Life

Faith Beats Fear: Inspiring Stories and Bible Scriptures to Strengthen Your Faith and Stop Fear Before It Stops You

A Holiday Reunion

Happily Ever Christmas

Connect With Author

https://www.lakeshiapoole.com

https://www.youtube.com/@lakeshiapoole

Author's Note

"I don't know what to say."

Part whisper, part heavy sigh, this is how my early morning began. I wanted to pray. A tornado of thoughts spun round and round in my mind, wreaking havoc. Memories and regrets were uprooted. Yet-to-be, unfulfilled dreams tossed from here to there. The chaotic brainstorm went a little like this.

I need to do this. You shouldn't have done that. I really want this, but it doesn't look likely. Why is this happening? What if that happens? Wait, what will 'they' think about me when I do this?

No scriptures, positive affirmations, or neat Christian-sounding phrases immediately popped up in response to the barrage of questions.

I was already exhausted, though the day had barely begun. Maybe I could just go back to sleep and ignore the relentless thoughts.

A sliver of light cut through my bedroom, but everything around me still seemed so dark. I felt heavy, burdened by questions I didn't have answers to.

1

I'm supposed to pray. I have to pray. This I knew. But...*I don't know what to say. Like, I don't even know what to ask.*

I wrote these prayers for moments like that – for others who deep down know they need to pray, but have no idea where to start.

Here. Take some of my words.

I've been where you are and am so grateful for the writers who gave me their words in my time of need. As Proverbs 16:24 tells us, "Gracious words are like a honeycomb, sweetness to the soul and health to the body."

That's what I want for you. That's my gift to you! These are *our* prayers.

Because here's the key that unlocked so much for me when it comes to prayer. It is less about the what and all about the Who. Prayer is about the presence of God. These prayers all point you back to God.

I prayed about which words to include, which aspects of purpose would be necessary for this season to address. I asked God to guide me as I wrote, to fill these pages with what He knows you need.

Honestly, I'm a little surprised by some of the prayers. When we talk about purpose, it's often wrapped up in a carefree, motivational message. But through life's twists and turns, God has shown me that purpose isn't always a straightforward, easy route. Purpose isn't this fun, Instagrammable, top-of-the-mountain moment every time. Sometimes, it weighs heavy. Sometimes, it's a quiet persistence, a daily search for meaning in the middle of a mess.

These prayers are for those who, like me, have wrestled with purpose–sometimes to the point of wanting to tap out. They're for the ones who have found themselves desperately searching for what truly matters. For the ones who don't have all the answers, and struggle to find the words to speak.

When you're in seasons like this, I don't want you to ever shut out the One who can guide you simply because you don't know what to say.

So take these prayers. They're imperfect like we all are, but they're ours. Let them encourage and edify you as you navigate your own path of purpose. And remember, you're not alone. We are in this journey together—praying, seeking, and trusting in an Almighty God who holds our purpose in His hands.

Introduction

I am smiling so big right now! I get to go with you on this transformative journey that will guide you through 31 days of dedicated prayer. I know the extraordinary results that come when we pray together, so I truly count it a privilege and honor to join you, friend.

You may see yourself as one individual seeking more of God for yourself. But I have to take a moment to point out you are not alone. So many others–including me–are in prayer right alongside you. Also, your prayers of purpose have the potential to affect not just you but your family, neighborhood, workplace, country, and the whole world.

Do you see what's happening in this world? In our communities? In our schools? We need you to pray. We need you to move in your purpose.

Each day you're granted opportunities to be an answered prayer in someone's life. The simplest kindness—a hello, helpful word of advice, or even a hug—brings light and hope into everyday situations that others are struggling through. There are people who are waiting for you to use your gifts, talents, and experience to offer a solution that eliminates their issues. What you have is just that special. I pray that you begin to see and believe that over the next few weeks.

This mission is not one we are meant to achieve alone. While so many people and things demand our attention and affection, almost to the point of overwhelm, we can find help in the Lord. We establish a rhythm of peace and purpose by prioritizing spiritual growth and development. That's where this guide comes in!

Prayer is not just a ritual but a lifeline—it is a sacred space where we connect deeply with the One who sees, loves, and perfects us. It is through prayer that we seek wisdom, peace, and alignment with God's will for our lives.

In these quiet, intimate moments, we learn that purpose is not something to be chased or earned, but revealed and lived out daily through our relationship with God. We lean on prayer as a first response and not a last resort to navigate both life's challenges and victories.

Count each moment of prayer as an opportunity to still yourself in the powerful, peace-giving presence of God, your Helper, your Keeper.

I lift up my eyes to the hills. From where does my help come?
My help comes from the Lord, who made heaven and earth.

— Psalm 121:1-2

Discovering Your Purpose Through Daily Prayer

Now, this guide is designed specifically for anyone yearning to find and operate in their purpose. Let me just say, I feel like that word gets thrown around so much these days. The search for "purpose" can begin to feel like the longest treasure hunt ever.

But as children of God, we are to recognize that everything, including our purpose and daily priorities, comes from God. We also exhibit a desire to align whatever we think or do with God's will and ways.

So before we get too deep into the prayers, friend, I want you to breathe. To pause. To relieve yourself of the pressures weighing heavy on your shoulders. I don't care if you put them there or the world did–release the ideas around purpose that have you feeling like you're always falling short and not good enough. Let go of the jealousy and envy you have against others who seem to have it all together. Stop attempting to copy and paste somebody else's lifestyle and choices because it *seems* like they have this purpose thing down and you're lost.

Breathe. Pause. Relieve. Release. Let go. Stop.

All of that stuff adds more stress and strain to your life than you realize. Overdoing it and playing the comparison game will have you looking in all the wrong places for purpose. These prayers will point you to the originator of purpose: God, your Creator.

In the next few pages, you will find prayers that will encourage you to discover purpose in the big and boring aspects of life. I've also included inspirational quotes about purpose. Let's glean from these personal insights as we pray with purpose.

Listen, it all matters. Every single piece of your life.

Society often discusses purpose as something elusive and grandiose. Yet, the truth is that purpose is connected to your daily beliefs, actions, and decisions. It's in these everyday moments that you find the path to a deeper understanding of God's will for your life. You discover God's *ways* as you experience daily life—as you show up for your family and at your job, certain character traits are being developed within you. You are gaining skills and relationships that come together for your good and God's purpose.

However, if you underestimate the importance of these tasks and moments, your pride may convince you that they're meaningless, and you'll miss so many God appointments and assignments, aka *purpose*.

As long as we make purpose into this impractical, abstract thing looming over our lives, we will overlook the patterns of purpose God reveals each day. We ignore opportunities to be who God called us to be when we go to work, stop by the grocery store, meet with family and friends, and do our daily duties.

It's no wonder that we find ourselves bored and perhaps even resentful of our routines. We don't perceive them to be critical parts of our God-ordained purpose-development.

If you've ever wondered if God has a purpose for your life, the answer is yes. And that purpose shows up every day. The goal of this resource is to help you show up with purpose every day too! I want you to see it, just like God opened Hagar's eyes to see the well in the wilderness in Genesis 21:19. Maybe life has you feeling like you're in a wilderness of your own. You're wandering aimlessly from one day to the next, wondering if God cares.

Not only does God care, but God is orchestrating so much on your behalf so that His kingdom may come to earth. You play a critical role in that happening and understanding your everyday purpose is a must.

Why Is it So Hard to Figure Out My Purpose?

We must discern between the allure of worldly priorities and comforts vs. the authentic call of God's purpose. In many spaces, purpose is presented as this feel-good experience where everything is perfect, nothing goes wrong, you make a lot of money and everybody loves you. Here's the thing, purpose isn't always comfortable, and it's not always about *you*.

Let me explain. Yes, God cares so much about you and your personal life and goals. But can I be honest? God also cares a lot about the kingdom and divine purpose. This is not to say that you should downplay your personal dreams, but I hope that after the next 31 days, you will see more clearly how the gifts, opportunities, and talents God has bestowed you with are part of a larger plan for all of God's people.

You are not alone or meant to operate in a silo, but in community.

We need you to be committed to God's will and ways because all of our lives are interconnected. This is why comparison and competition are serious purpose killers — I promise you there's room for all of us!

Take a moment to envision the numerous others who are joining you on this journey. Not only am I right here with you, but they are too. Can you imagine the mountains our collective prayers are moving? I get goosebumps thinking about how we are all building our purpose on prayer. That means we will be effective. That means what we do will last for generations to come.

Made By God, Purposed By God

So often when we seek out spiritual growth and development we strike out on our own as if we know the way. We may seek the support and guidance of a pastor, church, or perhaps even Christian books. These are all wonderful resources. However, your greatest Guide is your God. Prayer gives you the opportunity to go before God and get the best information straight from the source.

Think about it – when you want to know about how something works, the best person to ask is the one who designed or created it. The same goes for us.

There is a passage in Jeremiah 33:2-3 that really resonated with me:

"Thus says the Lord who made the earth, the Lord who formed it to establish it—the Lord is his name: Call to me and I will answer you, and will tell you great and hidden things that you have not known."

Here's the context. God is speaking to the prophet Jeremiah, promising peace and restoration to Jerusalem and Judah, even though they are currently in a state of devastation due to their sins and the ongoing siege by the Chaldeans.

I want you to pay particular attention to how the Bible clearly states that the Lord made the earth, formed it, and established it. The Bible often reminds us of who God is—the One who made the world. Sometimes, we need to remember that God made us, too. In fact, we were made in God's image and likeness (Genesis 1:26-27).

As part of this Creator-creation relationship, we can go to our Lord to learn "great and hidden things". If you've been in search of clarity and understanding around your purpose, praying to God should be your first stop.

It's also worth noting that as those confessing Jesus Christ, we are being *made* to mirror our Savior, too. Not only was our original design meant to reflect God, but as new creations in Christ we are being made, day-by-day. To operate with the mind of Christ. To display the fruit of the Spirit. This is the purpose development we're engaged in on a daily basis.

Prayer simply positions and prepares you to become who God designed you to be.

Purpose Beyond Self

A lot of spiritual development resources focus on how you can be a better Christian and on self-improvement, which is great. However, it can create a very self-centered faith journey where you only commit to actions that you believe will make you and your life better. However, Jesus commands us to be about more than ourselves.

In Matthew 22:36-40, Jesus is asked which is the greatest commandment. He answered: "You shall love the Lord your God with all your heart and with all your soul and with all your mind. This is the great and first commandment. And a second is like it: You shall love your neighbor as yourself. On these two commandments depend all the Law and the Prophets."

At the heart of our purpose is the commandment to love. To love God, love ourselves, and love our neighbors. These guided prayers will show you how you can live out this commandment through your purpose.

Why Do I Struggle In My Prayer Life?

Do you believe that prayer works? No, seriously. I think a lot of us say we believe because it's the Christian thing to say/do, but if you look at some of our actions, we don't trust in prayer as an effective way to live life. Google or Facebook gets more trust as we seek out answers.

I don't say this to make you feel guilty or to condemn you but to help you set the right expectations. Don't judge prayer's effectiveness by getting specifically what you want. It is not rendered ineffective because you do not like or enjoy God's answer. When it comes to purpose, remember this is about God's purpose for our lives and His kingdom. God is not a genie waiting to act at our commands. Prayer is about becoming more aware of God's presence and building trust and a relationship.

As you embark on this 31-day journey, I pray your belief in the power and effectiveness of prayer is multiplied. I hope that you feel emboldened by approaching God's throne. No, you don't deserve the opportunity to command an audience before the King each day, but as a child of the Most High, this is your royal privilege.

Each day's prayer is a step towards understanding your unique role in the kingdom of God. I encourage you to treat each prayer as a starting point. Don't just read the words. Meditate on the ideas presented and receive any divine assignments or revelations as part of your daily fill-up of living water (John 4:14). Believe and live what you say!

A Journey of Discovery

As you turn each page, let it be an invitation to discover not just the purpose God has for you, but the kingdom.

When you reflect on your life experiences and the people you've met, you will begin to see how God has been weaving together your unique path to purpose all along.

You were never alone. You were never forgotten. You were never forsaken.

It's okay if you just couldn't see it in the past. Ask God to keep showing you more and more of Himself. Pray for God to make you more sensitive and aware of how He sees you.

The subtitle for this guide is "31 Prayers to Encourage and Empower You to Stay Connected and Committed to God's Will & Way." It's a little wordy, I know, but it was very important to me to include every single word.

Prayer is encouraging and empowering. At least it should be. If you've struggled with establishing a prayer life in the past, your perception may be tainted. Please don't see it as drudgery or some obligation you dread doing. Decide right now: *I will be encouraged and empowered by praying*.

I also wanted to show you how prayer is a way to stay connected and committed. The journey of faith is one with many ups and downs. Prayer allows you to hold onto God's word and promises. It also is a critical part of building a strong relationship with the Lover of your soul and others. Prayer is a connection point for the Presence of God. In those moments you feel like giving up or as if life is too much, prayer can give you that extra motivation to push through.

Last but not least, when it comes to commitment, we have to be cognizant of where we're devoting our time and energy – what are you really prioritizing? Committing ourselves to God's will and way means putting the kingdom first. Not only is there a very specific plan (will) but there is a divine approach (way) that we should consider. Prayer is how we gain the wisdom, insight, clarity, and direction.

This book is not just a collection of prayers. It is a pathway to discovering how every single step we take, day by day shapes our ultimate purpose. It's up to us to be active participants. I pray you embrace this journey with an open heart, and let each prayer prompt you to lean in closer to God—the One who sees you, loves you, and makes you whole.

Day 1

DEAR GOD, I turn my attention and my heart to You. You are my Creator and the One who made heaven and earth with such beautiful detail. I know purpose is a part of everything You designed, including *me*.

I am Your child. Your love, grace, and mercy are everlasting, carrying me from moment to moment. Thank You for always being with me, never leaving or abandoning me as You promised. I am grateful.

When the world around me feels overwhelming, gently remind me of Your presence. Reassure me that even in the midst of uncertainty and the trials that shadow my days, Your goodness towards me remains unchanged. You have a purpose for my life. Shine the light on who I am and what You would have me to do today.

If I'm being honest, sometimes I have been confused and frustrated. I have wondered why you brought me to this point and place in my life. God, where there is pain, I pray I find divine comfort. You can transform anything and anybody. Cleanse my heart and set my mind on You so that I may be who You created me to be.

In Your divine wisdom, You weave together every thread of my experiences—the good and the bad, the wins and the losses, the pain and the proud moments—as part of Your bigger purpose. Make my will one with Yours.

Today, help me trust in what You're doing in and around me, knowing that everything, through Your power, is being worked out for my good and for Your greater plan.

AMEN.

And we know that for those who love God all things work together for good, for those who are called according to his purpose.

— Romans 8:28 (ESV)

Responsive Reflections

Journal about any thoughts or ideas that come to mind in response to today's prayer and Bible passage.

_____

_____

_____

_____

_____

_____

_____

_____

_____

_____

_____

_____

The whole purpose of our prayer is concentrated into the sight and contemplation of him to whom we pray, feeling marvellous joy, reverent fear and such great sweetness and delight in him that at that moment we can only pray as he moves us.

JULIAN OF NORWICH

Day 2

DEAR GOD, I come before You, seeking wisdom and understanding about the divine purpose You have destined for me and Your people. I am reminded that You have made everything for a purpose — a testament to Your sovereignty. God, you are at work in the earth. How can I join you?

I acknowledge that my understanding is limited — I don't know all the details or why things are happening this way. There are times when I worry and doubt that any good will come my way. I question when what I plan falls apart, not realizing that Your purpose always prevails. That may mean that sometimes your answers to my prayers are no and not yet. Remind me that You know best, and much better than me.

Forgive me for thinking I know best and trying to control or force things to go my way. Thank You for teaching me how to let go and trust You.

Show me how You see me—as someone who is loved and under the care of a Father. I don't have to figure everything out on my own. When I try to jump ahead of You or do things my way, I end up distancing myself from You, and I don't want to do that anymore. Help me realize I don't need to come up with my own plans to save myself—I can always turn to You.

Today, help me take on the roles and responsibilities You've assigned me, knowing that even the smallest things, when done in line with Your will, have lasting importance.

AMEN.

No one who trusts in you will ever be disgraced, but disgrace comes to those who try to deceive others. Show me the right path, O Lord; point out the road for me to follow. Lead me by your truth and teach me, for you are the God who saves me. All day long I put my hope in you. Remember, O Lord, your compassion and unfailing love, which you have shown from long ages past.

— Psalm 25:3-6 (NLT)

RESPONSIVE REFLECTIONS

*Journal about any thoughts or ideas that come to mind in
response to today's prayer and Bible passage.*

_____

_____

_____

_____

_____

_____

_____

_____

_____

_____

_____

_____

_____

Prayer isn't just asking for things; it's an act of surrender. We place our worries, fears, dreams, and questions in God's hands and let go.

LARA CASEY

Day 3

DEAR GOD, I am grateful for the opportunity to approach Your throne. As an all-knowing Father, I can gain the right insight to shift my mind, heart, and actions. I am reminded that Your divine timing is everything.

In moments of impatience and seasons of waiting, strengthen my faith so that I may persevere and allow patience to have its perfect work. Help me to cling to the hope that every promise You have made will come to pass based on Your schedule.

Encourage my heart to find peace in the waiting, knowing that what may seem delayed or slow to me is all part of Your perfect plan. Help me not to overlook the small tasks while I wait for the "big" opportunity. Show me how the little steps lead the way. Guide me in learning the purpose of waiting with expectation.

I don't want to just sit back and do nothing—I want to draw closer to You, learning more about who You are and what You have in store for me. Lord, give me the grace to be patient, the faith to stay strong, and the ability to see Your hand in everything. Keep me grounded in the truth that purpose is always there, even when I can't fully see it.

Today, I choose to have a calm and trusting heart, knowing that everything God said will be fulfilled.

AMEN.

This vision is for a future time. It describes the end, and it will be fulfilled. If it seems slow in coming, wait patiently, for it will surely take place. It will not be delayed.

— Habakkuk 2:3 (NLT)

Responsive Reflections

Journal about any thoughts or ideas that come to mind in response to today's prayer and Bible passage.

_____

_____

_____

_____

_____

_____

_____

_____

_____

_____

_____

_____

Find out what God is doing, jump in the river of His will, and flow with the current of His plans.

CHRYSTAL EVANS

Day 4

DEAR GOD, I turn my heart towards You, seeking to deepen my trust in Your divine plan. I know I cannot do this on my own. As I face life's uncertainties and challenges, I choose to rely on Your leadership and lovingkindness. Lead me in this day. When I have to make a choice on which direction to go, speak to me, show me the righteous way. I want to make decisions with You in mind.

Help me, God. Teach me to trust in Your timing, Your ways, and Your promises. I find comfort in knowing that You are always with me, guiding my steps and providing a way for me. I am not alone. I am not too far out of your reach.

I want to remain faithful to You and Your purpose, even when confronted by adversity, conflict, and obstacles. Fill me with a peace that surpasses all understanding. Hide me under the cover of your protection and preserve my sanity and soul. Keep my mind and heart clear.

I know that You are for me and want to help me live purposefully. Because of Your presence, I have what it takes to be victorious, so I refuse to believe any negative thought or accusation that says otherwise. Quiet the noise in and around me that distracts me from being who You called me to be. Block out the critics who doubt You and the work You are doing in my life.

Today, I will walk in confidence, knowing that You reign supreme—nothing or no one (not even me) can stop the prosperity and purpose You have established for me.

AMEN.

You will keep in perfect peace all who trust in you, all whose thoughts are fixed on you! Trust in the Lord always, for the Lord God is the eternal Rock...But for those who are righteous, the way is not steep and rough. You are a God who does what is right, and you smooth out the path ahead of them. Lord, we show our trust in you by obeying your laws; our heart's desire is to glorify your name.

— Isaiah 26:3-4, 7-8 (NLT)

Responsive Reflections

*Journal about any thoughts or ideas that come to mind in
response to today's prayer and Bible passage.*

_____

_____

_____

_____

_____

_____

_____

_____

_____

_____

_____

_____

Preachers, teachers, servants of God don't you surrender your identity. Whether they believe you or not, you better know who you are.

PRATHIA HALL

Day 5

DEAR GOD, Sometimes my heart is heavy, and my trust in others feels shattered. I feel like I can't depend on anybody except myself. Remind me that I can always depend on You and that I shouldn't try to do everything on my own. In times of pain and confusion, Jesus, remind me that I can turn to You, a faithful and true Friend.

I know that to move forward in purpose, I've got to heal from the past —the hurtful words and actions that still hold me back. I need You, Jesus, to heal my heart and guide me through this. Show me anyone I still need to forgive. I pray my heart overflows with Your grace and mercy so that I may extend the same forgiveness to each of them.

Lord, please guide me through these emotions and thoughts that keep me from being who You designed me to be. Freedom is in forgiveness and I want to be free to follow my purpose fully.

Fill me up and refresh my spirit. Help me trust again—not just in myself or the people around me, but most of all, in You. Remind me that Your plans are always good, and that You'll never leave me, especially when life feels lonely. Send help! Allow me to discern and focus on those who are for me more than those who seem to be against me.

Give me the ability to see the good in others. Open my eyes and heart to see people and situations the way You do, so I can show grace, empathy, and compassion. You've got me covered and protect my heart, so I don't need to feel insecure, shut down, or close myself off. I won't turn to self-preservation or selfishness to keep me safe; I turn to You.

Today, I'm choosing to rest in Your protection, peace, and power.

AMEN.

Seek the Lord and his strength; seek his presence continually! Remember the wondrous works that he has done, his miracles, and the judgments he uttered

— Psalm 105:4-5 (ESV)

RESPONSIVE REFLECTIONS

Journal about any thoughts or ideas that come to mind in response to today's prayer and Bible passage.

Holding our hand is God's delight ...Getting there, even to some noble goal, is not as important to God, I suspect, as the journey in companionship with him. It's relationship, not achievement, that he wants.

ELIZABETH SHERRILL

Day 6

DEAR GOD, I need You. I seek Your presence and draw strength from Your promises and the prayers You've already answered. As I go on this journey of purpose, I find that sometimes it can be quite difficult and require a lot of sacrifices. Unexpected challenges cause heartache. Some days, I feel like I'm losing and it's hard to see the victories.

This makes me want to give in or give up, especially when my purpose isn't popular. Remind me that I am victorious through Jesus Christ alone. I want to see "wins" and "losses" as You see them. I refuse to surrender my soul to gain the world.

Help me recognize the cost of discipleship, and the importance of self-denial and faith. The problems I experience don't automatically mean that there's something wrong with me or that I'm not good enough; they could be the "trouble of the world" Jesus warned us about.

Lord, You are my Helper and my strength. When the weight of following Jesus Christ bears heavily upon me, I turn to You. Grant me the courage to take on the challenges that come with following in His footsteps and to carry my cross with humility and endurance.

Teach me to count the cost, not in worldly terms but through the lens of eternal grace and salvation. I want to be content in the promise of Your kingdom, a treasure far surpassing any earthly gain.

Today, I pray for wisdom to discern the right path and for a heart that rejoices in the privilege of being with You.

AMEN.

Then he said to the crowd, "If any of you wants to be my follower, you must give up your own way, take up your cross daily, and follow me. If you try to hang on to your life, you will lose it. But if you give up your life for my sake, you will save it. And what do you benefit if you gain the whole world but are yourself lost or destroyed?

— Luke 9:23-25 (NLT)

RESPONSIVE REFLECTIONS

*Journal about any thoughts or ideas that come to mind in
response to today's prayer and Bible passage.*

It may appear like an ordinary day, feel like just another trip to the store, or sound like just another task to complete. Listen with spiritual ears and look with spiritual eyes beyond what is happening in your life.

VASHTI MURPHY MCKENZIE

Day 7

DEAR GOD, When you prompt me to leave the former desires, pleasures, beliefs, and plans that do not align with Your purpose, help me to welcome the new things with wisdom and excitement.

Help me release the burdens of my past, let go of what once was, and accept the new work You are doing in my life.

You are making me into who I was always meant to be. I realize this is not an overnight transformation. There may be times when I mourn what is lost – comfort me Holy Spirit! Change is scary, so when I am uncertain or fear the new life you are preparing me for, please help me to cling to You.

When my situation feels hopeless, help me see You at work, bringing forth life and light where despair once lingered. I am grateful that You continue to perfect us in imperfect circumstances.

Teach me to perceive the new things You are creating today. With You, every situation is an opportunity for You to display Your power and love. There may be some things I've been dealing with for years, but You can renew and change it all.

In every challenge, remind me that You are doing something new, not just around me but within me.

Today, shape my heart and mind so that I may embrace Your changes with gratitude and holy expectation.

AMEN.

Delight yourself in the Lord, and he will give you the desires of your heart. Commit your way to the Lord; trust in him, and he will act.

— Psalm 37:4-5 (ESV)

RESPONSIVE REFLECTIONS

*Journal about any thoughts or ideas that come to mind in
response to today's prayer and Bible passage.*

God's purposes always have far more to do with your long-term sanctification than your short-term gratification.

PRISCILLA SHIRER

Day 8

DEAR GOD, I confess that at times I am tempted to rely on my understanding to follow the way I deem right. I base my assessment on the world's definition of success. Yet, Your Word teaches me to trust wholly in You, to lean not on my limited perspective but on Your infinite wisdom. I lay down my plans at Your feet, and surrender my will to Yours.

As the Creator of the universe and me, you have all the authority. I acknowledge You in all my ways so that I may be purposeful every day. May my thoughts, actions, and decisions reflect my trust in You. In moments of uncertainty, remind me of Your everlasting love and long-suffering nature. You pursue me. You wait for me. You are willing to leave the 99 for me. You never wish for me to fail or faint.

I pray I have faith, and listen for my Shepherd's voice before making a choice.

I will not be discouraged but will have the courage to follow where You lead, even when the path seems unclear or a waste of time. Instill in me a deep sense of peace, knowing that as I acknowledge You in all things, You will direct my steps, making my paths straight and smooth. Thank You for being my compass and my guide in purpose.

Today, I will trust in You not just with words, but through my actions and decisions.

AMEN.

Trust in the Lord with all your heart, and do not lean on your own understanding. In all your ways acknowledge him, and he will make straight your paths. Be not wise in your own eyes; fear the Lord, and turn away from evil.

— Proverbs 3:5-7 (ESV)

Responsive Reflections

Journal about any thoughts or ideas that come to mind in response to today's prayer and Bible passage.

_____

_____

_____

_____

_____

_____

_____

_____

_____

_____

_____

_____

_____

God's promise is, that He will take possession of our will, and work it for us, and that His suggestions will come to us, not so much commands from the outside, as desires springing up within. At once the matter should be committed to the Lord, with an instant consent of the will to obey Him.

HANNAH WHITALL SMITH

Day 9

DEAR GOD, Please guide me in this journey of discovering and pursuing the purpose You have designed for me. Bring to my mind the talents and gifts You have instilled in me and the experiences that have prepared me for this season of my life.

There may be ideas from the past or unfulfilled dreams that I'd given up on – give me a fresh wind for those things that align with Your purpose.

Help me to work heartily in all that I do, not for my own gain or the approval of others, but as an offering to You. In each task, big or small, let me find joy and purpose, knowing that I am ultimately serving You.

In moments of doubt or confusion, when the path ahead seems unclear, remind me of Your presence and guidance. Let Your Word be a lamp unto my feet, illuminating the way as I strive to align my ambitions and actions with Your divine will.

Create in me a spirit of perseverance and dedication. I don't want to just discover my calling. I also fully commit to it with all my heart, trusting that in doing so, I will find true fulfillment and abundance. You are a God who rewards those who diligently seek Your will.

Thank You for the assurance that as You work in me, and I look more like You, my efforts are never in vain.

Today, I desire to use all of me to glorify You.

AMEN.

And it is impossible to please God without faith. Anyone who wants to come to him must believe that God exists and that he rewards those who sincerely seek him.

— Hebrews 11:6 (NLT)

RESPONSIVE REFLECTIONS

Journal about any thoughts or ideas that come to mind in response to today's prayer and Bible passage.

There's nothing wrong with not having figured out who you are, but so much can go wrong when you pretend that you have.

SARAH JAKES ROBERTS

Day 10

DEAR GOD, I thank You for Your faithfulness and grace. I admit that there have been times when doubt clouded my trust in You. I ignored and neglected your assignments and instructions. I questioned Your plan, Your presence in my life, and even Your heart for me.

I ask for Your forgiveness and that Your lovingkindness would lead me to repentance. I am grateful for Your mercy. You welcome me back.

God, restore the time lost and missed opportunities that occurred due to poor stewardship of Your purpose. Forgive me for the procrastination, delayed obedience, and the ways I disrespected your sovereignty. I seek Your help to overcome my doubts and grow in reliance on You. Help me to accept Your grace and not allow my past to haunt and torment me but serve simply as lessons learned.

Teach me to rest in the assurance of Your promise to always be with me. You never waver in your love for me and your track record proves that You are a good and merciful God. Help me to wait patiently for Your timing, understanding that You see the bigger picture of my life. You withhold no good thing. When you correct and discipline me, I know that ultimately, the experience will make me better. I refuse to wallow in condemnation.

Help me overcome the urge to put off things I can do today until tomorrow—I don't want to assume I have more time. Remind me that even small steps are progress in Your plan. Strengthen my resolve to use each day for Your purpose, trusting that it's never too late to begin again.

Today, I will take action and step forward in faith, no longer delaying what You've called me to do.

AMEN.

Search me, O God, and know my heart! Try me and know my thoughts! And see if there be any grievous way in me, and lead me in the way everlasting!

— Psalm 139:23-24 (ESV)

RESPONSIVE REFLECTIONS

Journal about any thoughts or ideas that come to mind in response to today's prayer and Bible passage.

_____

_____

_____

_____

_____

_____

_____

_____

_____

_____

_____

_____

_____

Do the work your soul must have.

KATIE CANNON

Day 11

DEAR GOD, I seek to be more purposeful in my life, to truly display faith in You and Your ways. I want to fully commit to You. Help me find my greatest satisfaction in Your presence, Your Word, and the path You have laid out for me.

I ask that You would shape my heart's desires to reflect Your will. Let my aspirations and dreams be a reflection of Your purpose for my life and Your kingdom.

Teach me to recognize what beliefs, ideas, tasks and to-do's align with Your will and what does not. Give me the courage to let go of dreams and desires that are not of You, even the "good" things. I want to prioritize "God" things. Counsel and comfort me in grieving the loss of whatever life I thought I'd have.

Give me a clear mind and a loyal heart that's strong enough to resist distractions and temptations. I'm done wearing myself out with things You never asked me to do. I'm letting go of my people-pleasing ways that have left me drained and unavailable for Your purpose. From now on, I choose to focus on pleasing You.

Help me to recognize Your voice, even with all the noise around me. Whether it's big decisions or small ones, I want to keep coming to You for guidance. I just want to honor You in everything I do.

Today, I commit to placing You first and prioritizing Your voice, Your direction, and Your glory in every aspect of my life.

AMEN.

"So don't worry about these things, saying, 'What will we eat? What will we drink? What will we wear?' These things dominate the thoughts of unbelievers, but your heavenly Father already knows all your needs. Seek the Kingdom of God above all else, and live righteously, and he will give you everything you need. "So don't worry about tomorrow, for tomorrow will bring its own worries. Today's trouble is enough for today.

— Matthew 6:31-34 (NLT)

RESPONSIVE REFLECTIONS

Journal about any thoughts or ideas that come to mind in response to today's prayer and Bible passage.

Will you not, before venturing away from your early quiet hour, "commit thy works" to Him definitely, the special things you have to do today, and the unforeseen work which He may add in the course of it?

FRANCES RIDLEY HAVERGAL

Day 12

DEAR GOD, As I study Your Word, I want to find the inspiration and instruction to be purposeful. I ask for the insight to learn from the faithful servants who have gone before me. May their lives and testimonies inspire and instruct me in my own journey of faith. Help me to see the purpose and calling You placed in their lives and to draw parallels to my own path.

Grant me the wisdom to understand the lessons they learned, the challenges they overcame, and the faith they exhibited. Let their stories be a source of guidance and encouragement as I seek to find my purpose in You.

I want to be motivated to follow Jesus Christ. Help me to grasp the depths of Your truths and to apply them in my life. May Your Holy Spirit guide me into all truth, revealing the relevance of these ancient stories in my current circumstances.

Help me, Lord, to be purposeful in my Bible study, not merely seeking knowledge but to *know* You intimately. To get to know myself. I pray my heart burns for how You open up the scriptures to me and reveal Your way. Thank You for the gift of Your Word, a light along my path of purpose.

Today, I seek to draw closer to You, and take what I understand about Your word to walk in the path You have destined for me.

AMEN.

Joyful are people of integrity, who follow the instructions of the Lord...Oh, that my actions would consistently reflect your decrees! Then I will not be ashamed when I compare my life with your commands. As I learn your righteous regulations, I will thank you by living as I should!

— Psalm 119:1, 5-7 (NLT)

Responsive Reflections

Journal about any thoughts or ideas that come to mind in response to today's prayer and Bible passage.

_____

_____

_____

_____

_____

_____

_____

_____

_____

_____

_____

_____

_____

Through a diligent study of God's Word, under the guidance of His Spirit, you'll drop a strong anchor that will hold in the storms of life. You will know your God. And when you know your God, not only will you be strong, but you will do great exploits for Him.

KAY ARTHUR

Day 13

DEAR GOD, I am grateful for the opportunity to pray and to communicate with You. It is a privilege to consult the One who created heaven and earth. Lord, as I seek to understand my purpose and Your plan for my life, I acknowledge the vital role of prayer. Teach me to pray.

Remove any unbelief, false teaching, or misinterpretation about the power of prayer that keeps me from establishing a prayer life. I don't care what I've tried (and failed) in the past. Right now, it is a priority in my life.

Help me to see prayer not just as a way to ask for things, but as a way to really know You and discover who You created me to be. I want to rely on this conversation with You, not only for comfort but also as a powerful guide to help me discern and walk the path You've set for me. When I have questions or concerns, I want to come to You first, instead of trying to figure everything out on my own.

Every word I speak in Your presence is heard and valued. You listen. You care. You guide me. I don't want to hold anything back from You —my flaws and failures are safe in Your hands, and I trust You to use them as part of my purpose.

In times of uncertainty and searching, lead me to find clarity and direction through prayer. Help me to trust in Your answers, even when they don't match my expectations. Give me peace in knowing that Your plans are always for my good, even if I don't fully understand them.

Today, I trust that You are near, so when I call out, I will listen for Your voice and lean into Your kindness.

AMEN.

The Lord is righteous in all his ways and kind in all his works. The Lord is near to all who call on him, to all who call on him in truth.

— Psalm 145:17-18 (ESV)

RESPONSIVE REFLECTIONS

*Journal about any thoughts or ideas that come to mind in
response to today's prayer and Bible passage.*

I believe if we could only see before-hand what it is that our heavenly Father means us to be...if we could have a glimpse of this, we should not grudge all the trouble and pains He is taking with us now, to bring us up to that ideal, which is His thought of us.

ANNIE KEARY

Day 14

DEAR GOD, Lord, I know I can always depend on You to guide me with purpose. As I stand at a crossroads, unsure of what to do next, I'm asking for Your wisdom and direction. I refuse to let confusion keep me stuck or afraid, in Jesus' name.

I admit, it's hard sometimes to see past the challenges in front of me and imagine the future You have planned. But I know that everything with You is intentional. Even the little moments that seem insignificant to me matter to You, so help me to value them too. Let me lean on Your understanding instead of my own, trusting that You're leading me exactly where I need to go.

When the path ahead looks unfamiliar, remind me that You've already gone before me, preparing everything I'll need along the way. You are going along with me, and grace and mercy will follow me. Give me the courage to stand out and step up in faith, especially when I am purposed to break lifelong cycles and generational patterns that conflict with Your will. Forgive me for the times I've chosen tradition and comfort over following You.

Help me to believe what You say about me, not what others have said. When doubts and negative thoughts creep in, making me question whether I'm capable of doing what You've asked, I pray those thoughts are taken captive and replaced with the truth of who I am in Christ.

Today, I choose to move toward purpose, listening closely for your instructions.

AMEN.

Your own ears will hear him. Right behind you a voice will say, "This is the way you should go," whether to the right or to the left.

— Isaiah 30:21 (NLT)

Responsive Reflections

Journal about any thoughts or ideas that come to mind in response to today's prayer and Bible passage.

_____

_____

_____

_____

_____

_____

_____

_____

_____

_____

_____

_____

A hand shall sustain us and our daily burden, so that, smiling at yesterday's fears, we shall say, "This is easy, this is light." Ministries shall be assigned, and through our hands blessings shall be conveyed.

ELIZABETH RUNDELL CHARLES

Day 15

DEAR GOD, I am grateful for community, fellowship, friends, family, and people in my life. You know the desires of my heart and the path You have set for me. I seek allies and companions in this journey — family, friends, church members, colleagues, mentors, clients, and all those You have destined to walk alongside me. Guide me to individuals who will challenge, inspire, and encourage me to live out the purpose You have laid before me.

Lord, I'm asking for relationships that are rooted in Your love, where Your grace and wisdom shine through. Help me to build connections that not only bring joy but also honor You—where support and encouragement are at the heart of everything. When I don't get the support I expect, please protect me from feeling rejected and remind me to focus on You and the people who are truly there for me.

Surround me with people who are centered on You and driven by purpose—those who offer help, hope, and wise advice without hesitation. I know You might lead me out of my comfort zone to meet people with different backgrounds, and I pray I'm open to that, letting go of any judgments or assumptions I've made.

Help me be a source of encouragement to others. Teach me to listen with compassion, speak with kindness, and act with integrity. And please give me the time and space to nurture these important connections. With You, my relationships will be a source of strength, joy, and growth as I live on purpose.

Today, I will be fully present in moments of need and have the humility to accept help from others.

AMEN.

You didn't choose me. I chose you. I appointed you to go and produce lasting fruit, so that the Father will give you whatever you ask for, using my name. This is my command: Love each other.

— John 15:16-17 (NLT)

RESPONSIVE REFLECTIONS

*Journal about any thoughts or ideas that come to mind in
response to today's prayer and Bible passage.*

_____

_____

_____

_____

_____

_____

_____

_____

_____

_____

_____

_____

When we come together in unity and mutually respect and depend on each other's unique gifts, we begin to express the complete image of God in the earth.

MICHELLE MCCLAIN-WALTERS

Day 16

DEAR GOD, Over and over again in Your Word You tell us not to fear, but Lord it is hard sometimes. I confess that, at times, fear grips my heart, causing me to hesitate in pursuing opportunities. Forgive me for overlooking, rejecting, and avoiding the purpose You have for me. I ask for Your divine strength to overcome these fears, to trust in Your unfailing support and guidance.

Your Presence makes me bold and confident – remind me that I have You on my side. Grant me the courage to follow Your lead in pursuing goals and dreams that seem beyond my reach. With You, nothing is impossible.

At the same time, Lord, instill in me a spirit of humility to appreciate the little things and small opportunities. I don't want to underestimate the significance of these tasks, but approach them with the same dedication and commitment as the larger goals.

Fill me with joy and gratitude for every milestone and step forward. I praise You, not just for the outward blessings, but for the way You nurture and prosper my soul.

Today, replace my fear with faith, my doubt with determination, and my hesitation with heartfelt devotion to the path You created for me.

AMEN.

But Jesus looked at them and said, "With man this is impossible, but with God all things are possible." Then Peter said in reply, "See, we have left everything and followed you. What then will we have?" Jesus said to them, "Truly, I say to you, in the new world, when the Son of Man will sit on his glorious throne, you who have followed me will also sit on twelve thrones, judging the twelve tribes of Israel. And everyone who has left houses or brothers or sisters or father or mother or children or lands, for my name's sake, will receive a hundredfold and will inherit eternal life. But many who are first will be last, and the last first.

— Matthew 19:26-30 (ESV)

Responsive Reflections

Journal about any thoughts or ideas that come to mind in response to today's prayer and Bible passage.

_____

_____

_____

_____

_____

_____

_____

_____

_____

_____

_____

_____

_____

Courage is fear that has said its prayers and decided to go forward anyway.

JOYCE MEYER

Day 17

DEAR GOD, In this fast-paced world, where instant results are expected and desired, I find myself struggling with impatience, especially when my plans don't align with Your timeline. I recognize the need for Your wisdom and instruction to cultivate patience, to trust in Your perfect timing for all things.

Lord, help me understand the beauty and value of patience in the process. Remind me that every moment of waiting is an opportunity for growth and a chance to deepen my trust in You.

So much is happening within and around me during this waiting time —help me to notice and appreciate this inner work. Teach me to see waiting not as wasted time but as seasons full of potential for learning and spiritual growth. When I feel stuck or delayed, remind me of Your faithfulness and that Your promises are always perfectly timed.

I won't get tired of doing good. Instead, help me find joy and purpose in every step of this journey. Give me the strength to keep going with a joyful heart, knowing You're always working behind the scenes for my good.

When anxiety or frustration creeps in while I wait, bring me back to a place of peace and trust in You. I choose to believe that You will do exactly what You've promised, right on time.

Today, I will move forward with endurance and excitement for what's to come!

AMEN.

For you know that when your faith is tested, your endurance has a chance to grow. So let it grow, for when your endurance is fully developed, you will be perfect and complete, needing nothing. If you need wisdom, ask our generous God, and he will give it to you. He will not rebuke you for asking. But when you ask him, be sure that your faith is in God alone. Do not waver, for a person with divided loyalty is as unsettled as a wave of the sea that is blown and tossed by the wind.

— James 1:3-6 (NLT)

Responsive Reflections

Journal about any thoughts or ideas that come to mind in response to today's prayer and Bible passage.

_____

_____

_____

_____

_____

_____

_____

_____

_____

_____

_____

_____

Waiting captures a prayerful posture in our spirits of purposeful attentiveness toward God: looking toward him, longing for him. We wait upon him, not for what we hope to receive, but because of who he is. God is worthy to be waited on.

ALICIA BRITT CHOLE

Day 18

DEAR GOD, I've been through some disappointments that have made it hard to keep trusting. I thought things would work out a certain way, but they didn't, and it left me feeling like my life didn't have a purpose. I thought I was following what You wanted, but instead, I ended up hurt and uncomfortable.

Sometimes I don't even trust myself, other people, and if I'm honest, I don't trust You the way I should. It makes it hard to stay committed to Your purpose because I'm scared I'll end up in another painful situation.

I'm turning to You for the strength and resilience only You can give. Help me see these challenges not as setbacks, but as chances to grow and learn.

Give me the wisdom to accept the things, people, and situations I can't change. Surrendering to You, instead of trying to control everything, is the best way to handle disappointment. That's where I'll find my true purpose and experience Your Presence.

Strengthen me to face the future with confidence and to bounce back from setbacks, even stronger and more determined to follow the purpose You have for me. Help me let go of my disappointments and place them in Your caring hands, finding rest and renewal in You.

Today, I will look beyond the struggles of the moment and trust in the bigger picture of Your plan for my life.

AMEN.

Hear the voice of my pleas for mercy, when I cry to you for help, when I lift up my hands toward your most holy sanctuary...The Lord is my strength and my shield; in him my heart trusts, and I am helped; my heart exults, and with my song I give thanks to him. The Lord is the strength of his people; he is the saving refuge of his anointed.

— Psalm 28:2, 7-8 (ESV)

Responsive Reflections

Journal about any thoughts or ideas that come to mind in response to today's prayer and Bible passage.

There are parts of
our calling, works
of the Holy Spirit,
and defeats of the
darkness that will
come no other way
than through
furious, fervent,
faith-filled,
unceasing prayer.

BETH MOORE

Day 19

DEAR GOD, Help me stay committed, even when things get tough. Each day—no matter how tough—carries the potential for growth and purpose within Your divine plan.

There are some unexpected aspects of purpose that I don't always feel prepared for or excited about going through. Give me the strength to push through the trials and obstacles that come my way. Quiet the voice of the accuser and negative thoughts that attempt to condemn me or convince me to abandon Your will. I want to hear Your voice more clearly. Help me see challenges not as roadblocks, but as a green light to rely on You.

Teach me to find joy and hope along the way, knowing that the tests I face are refining me and shaping me into the person You want me to be.

Keep me focused on You. Instead of seeking to be perfect, I can trust that you are the One perfecting and preparing me.

Let me be inspired by those who have gone before me, who faced their own struggles and came out stronger in their walk with You. Bring to my mind words that they've said, prayers they've prayed, and actions that they've taken that could help me along the way. When You prompt people to encourage and share wisdom with me, open my ears and heart that I may listen well.

Today, I will press forward and take on this day with faith, hope, and determination.

AMEN.

We are human, but we don't wage war as humans do. We use God's mighty weapons, not worldly weapons, to knock down the strongholds of human reasoning and to destroy false arguments. We destroy every proud obstacle that keeps people from knowing God. We capture their rebellious thoughts and teach them to obey Christ.

— 2 Corinthians 10:3-5 (NLT)

RESPONSIVE REFLECTIONS

*Journal about any thoughts or ideas that come to mind in
response to today's prayer and Bible passage.*

_____

_____

_____

_____

_____

_____

_____

_____

_____

_____

_____

_____

A door may be closed so that God can have your attention and readiness for the better door to open. He is not finished.

MARSHAWN EVANS DANIELS

Day 20

DEAR GOD, I'm so grateful that even though You're so big and powerful, You still care about the small, everyday moments of my life. With You, the ordinary things become extraordinary and full of purpose. In a world that only seems to celebrate the big, flashy successes, help me see the beauty and importance of the little victories, the quiet progress, and the valleys I've made it through. Remind me that purpose starts with one small step at a time. Every great achievement begins with something simple.

Help me recognize the value in humble beginnings. Give me a heart that appreciates the process and finds joy in the journey, even when it feels slow and my progress goes unnoticed.

Guide me, Lord, as I take each step forward, trusting that You're with me every inch of the way. When I feel doubt creeping in or discouragement trying to pull me down, remind me that You see me. You celebrate who I am becoming. You're in the details, and You're working even in the tiniest parts of my life.

Help me see and understand that progress isn't always about big leaps, but sometimes it's about faithfully showing up, doing the work, and trusting *You* with the outcome. You will be responsible for the results, I need only to have faith and follow Your instructions. Thank You for being a God who cares about the big and the small.

Today, I will trust You with the "small" stuff, the ordinary, and expect Your transformative power to make a difference in my purpose.

AMEN.

Farmers who wait for perfect weather never plant. If they watch every cloud, they never harvest. Just as you cannot understand the path of the wind or the mystery of a tiny baby growing in its mother's womb, so you cannot understand the activity of God, who does all things. Plant your seed in the morning and keep busy all afternoon, for you don't know if profit will come from one activity or another—or maybe both.

— Ecclesiastes 11:4-6 (NLT)

Responsive Reflections

Journal about any thoughts or ideas that come to mind in response to today's prayer and Bible passage.

_____

_____

_____

_____

_____

_____

_____

_____

_____

_____

_____

_____

We have to pray with our eyes on God, not on the difficulties.

ELISABETH ELLIOT

Day 21

DEAR GOD, You are love, and You have called us to love. I realize that a key part of my purpose is reflecting that love through both my beliefs and my actions. Teach me what it truly means to serve others, and help me understand the blessings that come from loving You and loving others as I love myself.

Show me the depth of Your love through Your Word and in the way You've cared for Your people, generation after generation. Cleanse me of any self-hatred, and teach me to love and show compassion to myself. Remind me that loving myself is not selfish, but part of Your design. Guide me, Lord, to see the opportunities You place before me each day to show love to those around me.

Help me to understand that when I serve those You've called me to serve, I am serving You. In that service, I find a deeper sense of purpose and fulfillment. Give me a heart that is eager to give, compassionate to understand, and patient to endure.

Grant me the wisdom to recognize the needs of those around me, and provide me with the resources and strength to support them. Guide me, so that I don't become overwhelmed or burned out. Teach me to pour from the overflow of Your love, not from an empty cup. Remind me that each day, I need to fill up on You first!

Today, I will choose to love and serve, knowing that Your heart is my refuge and Your love is my foundation.

AMEN.

And you must love the Lord your God with all your heart, all your soul, all your mind, and all your strength.' The second is equally important: 'Love your neighbor as yourself.' No other commandment is greater than these."

— Mark 12:30-31 (NLT)

RESPONSIVE REFLECTIONS

Journal about any thoughts or ideas that come to mind in response to today's prayer and Bible passage.

_____

_____

_____

_____

_____

_____

_____

_____

_____

_____

_____

_____

_____

God loves us too much to answer our prayers at any other time than the right time and in any other way than the right way.

LYSA TERKEURST

Day 22

DEAR GOD, I ask for Your guidance and the confidence to open my heart and share my testimony — it may be in a small word of encouragement or a more formal opportunity that You've prepared for me.

My experiences aren't just for me. Sharing how You've changed my life can help others, too. Help me see the power in my story — the power to inspire, heal, and give hope to others who might be going through something similar.

Give me a heart full of empathy and compassion, so I'm willing to be vulnerable when You call me to be. Don't let shame, guilt, fear of judgment, rejection, or gossip hold me back from sharing Your glory with others. You cover me – including my past mistakes and short-comings – in love and grace.

Grant me the courage, Lord, to speak openly and truthfully. I want to be able to share the highs and lows, the struggles and victories, knowing that in doing so, I am not only finding healing for myself but also extending Your light to those who may be going through dark times. I don't want to hide Your light. I will be the light of the world as Jesus commanded.

Give me the right words and the wisdom to share my experiences in a way that honors You. Tell me when, where, and how. Let my story be a living testimony of Your goodness, encouraging others to seek You and find their own path to healing and purpose. Today, I won't be afraid or hesitate to tell others about Your goodness and the purpose You've given me.

AMEN.

Oh give thanks to the Lord; call upon his name; make known his deeds among the peoples!

— 1 Chronicles 16:8 (ESV)

Responsive Reflections

*Journal about any thoughts or ideas that come to mind in
response to today's prayer and Bible passage.*

_____

_____

_____

_____

_____

_____

_____

_____

_____

_____

_____

I have recorded how the Lord called me to his work, and how he has kept me from falling from grace, as I feared I should. In all things he has proved himself a God of truth to me.

JARENA LEE

Day 23

DEAR GOD, My heart is full of gratitude for Your promise to give strength to the weary and power to the weak. As I pursue the purpose You've set for me, I ask for Your divine energy and sustaining power to start, keep going, and complete what You've entrusted to me.

Whether it is showing up for my family, work, church, community, or any place You've sent me, I sometimes feel like I'm juggling too much. I want to do well and *be* well.

For the things I've taken on that don't serve me or You, I surrender them now. Help me see that stepping away isn't quitting or failing; it's making room to say yes to what You've truly called me to. When I focus on what You've ordained for me, You will empower me with supernatural strength to keep going.

Give me the wisdom and resources to take care of myself—physically, mentally, spiritually, and emotionally—so I can carry out my purpose with excellence. I embrace my weaknesses, knowing that Your power shows up perfectly in them. Help me see boundaries and limitations not as roadblocks but as chances to lean on You and discover what really matters in Your plan.

My ability to keep going doesn't rely just on my own strength, but on Your endless power.

Today, I turn to You to renew my strength and will keep moving forward with determination and dedication.

AMEN.

And let us not grow weary of doing good, for in due season we will reap, if we do not give up. So then, as we have opportunity, let us do good to everyone, and especially to those who are of the household of faith.

— Galatians 6:9-10 (ESV)

Responsive Reflections

Journal about any thoughts or ideas that come to mind in response to today's prayer and Bible passage.

_____

_____

_____

_____

_____

_____

_____

_____

_____

_____

_____

The good life isn't the absence of heartache; it's the presence of God, by grace, in the midst of it. Our hope in the midst of hardship is that Jesus doesn't just work things out for our good—he is our good.

RUTH CHOU SIMONS

Day 24

DEAR GOD, You are my Creator. Just as You do with everything, You designed me with purpose in mind from the very beginning. I praise You because everything You create is good. You, the One who made the universe and all its wonders, are the source of all knowledge and wisdom. I trust Your plan for my life because You know me better than anyone else.

Sometimes, I feel unsure of myself—my identity, my personality, and even what's true for me. Show me the person You want me to be, and help me let go of any thoughts or ideas that don't line up with that. Remind me that I am Your child, and I have a place in Your kingdom. I want to walk confidently in my true identity, knowing that in You, I am whole, loved, and full of purpose.

When I tried to be someone I'm not, forgive me. You've made me into Who I am purposefully. I am my best when I walk in my purpose authentically. In the moments where I compromised my integrity and future with You, have mercy on me. Restore me to wholeness and health, and show me who I truly am in Jesus Christ.

Help me to find joy in the simple, everyday tasks and responsibilities You've given me that help grow Your kingdom. Show me how being faithful in the small things opens the door for greater blessings to come.

Today, I choose to believe that being myself, the person You lovingly designed, is more than enough to fulfill my purpose.

AMEN.

Since you have been raised to new life with Christ, set your sights on the realities of heaven, where Christ sits in the place of honor at God's right hand. Think about the things of heaven, not the things of earth. For you died to this life, and your real life is hidden with Christ in God.

— Colossians 3:1-3 (NLT)

Responsive Reflections

Journal about any thoughts or ideas that come to mind in response to today's prayer and Bible passage.

_____

_____

_____

_____

_____

_____

_____

_____

_____

_____

_____

_____

You began as a vision in the Potter's heart before you took shape in his hands. Your unique value and identity were skillfully designed before you were formed. The divine Potter designs every person with a unique purpose according to his own vision of perfection.

NONA JONES

Day 25

DEAR GOD, I find confidence in knowing that my purpose is in Your hands. You're guiding me every step of the way, shaping me into who You've called me to be.

Lord, I'm committing myself to a journey of learning and spiritual growth. I know change doesn't happen overnight—it's a process that takes patience and perseverance. Help me see each day as an opportunity to become a little more like the person You've created me to be, whether that means growing in some areas or letting go of habits that do not serve You.

Holy Spirit, lead me. Show me the way forward, light my path, and teach me through every encounter. Give me the humility to keep learning from Your Word and Your ways. When I'm seeking understanding, help me not to rely on my own knowledge, but always to look to You for revelation. You are revealing my purpose day-by-day, moment-by-moment – open my eyes that I may see and my ears that I may hear and understand. Most importantly, help me take what I see and hear and *do* life Your way.

Give me the strength to keep going, especially when it feels like progress is slow or the path is hard. Remind me that You're always at work in me, even when life feels mundane or challenging. I want my life to be marked by Your presence, Lord. Keep my heart open to Your lessons and ready to receive Your guidance.

Today, I am eager to learn from the people and experiences God places in my life.

AMEN.

Get all the advice and instruction you can, so you will be wise the rest of your life. You can make many plans, but the Lord's purpose will prevail.

— Proverbs 19:20-21 (NLT)

Responsive Reflections

Journal about any thoughts or ideas that come to mind in response to today's prayer and Bible passage.

_____

_____

_____

_____

_____

_____

_____

_____

_____

_____

_____

_____

_____

My belief is that when you're telling the truth, you're close to God. So prayer is our sometimes real selves trying to communicate with the Real, with Truth, with the Light. It is us reaching out to be heard, hoping to be found by a light and warmth in the world, instead of darkness and cold.

ANNE LAMOTT

Day 26

DEAR GOD, I want to want what You want. As I seek to live a life of purpose, I know I need to align my goals with Your will for me. Lord, guide me through this transformation, helping me to understand and follow Your good, pleasing, and perfect will.

In a world where success is often measured by worldly standards, I ask for Your protection and perspective. Help me set goals that honor You, reflect my calling as Your child, and contribute to building Your kingdom.

I seek Your guidance in every decision and want my ambitions to focus on manifesting your glory in the earth.

Grant me a discerning heart to know what truly matters. Help me prioritize my life based on Your values and principles. Remind me of the fleeting nature of worldly success and keep me focused on the eternal impact of my words, actions, and choices.

As I set goals, encourage me to look beyond my own interests and consider the needs of others. Inspire me to pursue love, justice, and peace in all that I do.

Today, I set my heart on Your will, trusting that as I align my goals with Yours, You will guide my steps and lead me to a life of purpose and impact.

AMEN.

No, O people, the Lord has told you what is good, and this is what he requires of you: to do what is right, to love mercy, and to walk humbly with your God.

— Micah 6:8 (NLT)

RESPONSIVE REFLECTIONS

Journal about any thoughts or ideas that come to mind in response to today's prayer and Bible passage.

O Father! Help us to resign our hearts, our strength, our wills to Thee; Then even lowliest work of Thine most noble, blest, and sweet will be.

HARRIET MCEWEN KIMBALL

Day 27

DEAR GOD, Every moment counts with You. Guide me to a deeper understanding of the significance of every action, no matter how minor it may appear. Instill in me a spirit of gratitude for every milestone, big and small, acknowledging that each is a blessing from You and an opportunity to be who You created me to be.

Lord, I don't want to keep overlooking the little things, for in them I find countless opportunities to express Your love and grace. Remind me that by cherishing and celebrating these moments, I am offering praise and thanks to You for Your continuous guidance and care.

I ask for eyes that see the value in the small gestures of kindness, ears that hear the quiet words of encouragement, and a heart that feels the gentle touch of Your presence in everyday acts of goodness. May each small deed be a reflection of Your love and a step towards fulfilling the purpose You have set for me.

Encourage me, Father, to live each day with a heart full of gratitude, recognizing the blessings You bestow upon me. Let me never overlook the little things, for they are often the greatest expressions of Your presence in my life.

Today, I will cherish and celebrate every moment, knowing that in doing so, I am honoring You and walking in the purpose You have for me.

AMEN.

---

that the God of our Lord Jesus Christ, the Father of glory, may give you the Spirit of wisdom and of revelation in the knowledge of him, having the eyes of your hearts enlightened, that you may know what is the hope to which he has called you, what are the riches of his glorious inheritance in the saints, and what is the immeasurable greatness of his power toward us who believe, according to the working of his great might

— Ephesians 1:17-19 (ESV)

RESPONSIVE REFLECTIONS

Journal about any thoughts or ideas that come to mind in response to today's prayer and Bible passage.

_____

_____

_____

_____

_____

_____

_____

_____

_____

_____

_____

There is so much to be set right in the world, there are so many to be led and helped and comforted, that we must continually come in contact with such in our daily life. Let us only take care... we do not miss our turn of service, and pass by those whom we might have been sent on an errand straight from God.

ELIZABETH RUNDELL CHARLES

Day 28

DEAR GOD, I just want to say thank You for Your hand guiding me in every step of my path, from the smallest achievements to the greatest triumphs. There is a part of me that hesitates to celebrate because I am afraid that things may take a turn, but remind me that You are with me no matter what. I can smile and shout for joy because of You.

Thank You for guiding, supporting, and empowering me. Help me to recognize and appreciate the progress I have made, seeing each accomplishment as a testament to Your grace and love. What have I done lately that I overlooked or never celebrated? When I brush off success, I fail to honor Your promises fulfilled.

I reject false humility that downplays the talents, gifts, and opportunities You have given me.

In moments of success, protect me from the shadow of survivor's remorse, where I question why I have done well. Remind me that my achievements are not just for myself but are opportunities to demonstrate Your goodness and to inspire others. Teach me to use these moments to express my heartfelt gratitude to You and to share Your love with those around me.

Encourage me to celebrate these milestones with a spirit of thankfulness, knowing that every win is due to Your grace and mercy. I pray my achievements always lead me back to You in gratitude, not to myself in pride.

Today, I will display gratitude and excitement about my life without fear of my future or any potential challenges because I know that You will be with me no matter what.

AMEN.

Always be joyful. Never stop praying. Be thankful in all circumstances, for this is God's will for you who belong to Christ Jesus. Do not stifle the Holy Spirit.

— 1 Thessalonians 5:16-19 (NLT)

RESPONSIVE REFLECTIONS

Journal about any thoughts or ideas that come to mind in response to today's prayer and Bible passage.

_____

_____

_____

_____

_____

_____

_____

_____

_____

_____

_____

_____

Everything great and everything little seemed done in the same spirit, and with the same degree of fidelity, because it was the will of God; and that which could not be traced to His will was not undertaken at all.

MARY ANNE
SCHIMMELPENNINCK

Day 29

DEAR GOD, There are times on this journey when I feel my motivation slipping and my focus wandering. Please renew my commitment to the plan and the people You've placed in my life.

Help me stay motivated and dedicated to Your mission. I know that when I put You first, everything else will fall into place. Rekindle the passion and excitement in me for what You've entrusted to me. Let my heart be filled with a fresh sense of purpose and a clear vision of the path You want me to take.

When the road is filled with detours and unexpected challenges and the progress seems slow, remind me of the greatest prize: Your Presence. My purpose is not just in the fulfillment of earthly goals but in eternal life through Jesus Christ.

Jesus, I fix my eyes on You — the author and perfecter of my faith. In moments of doubt or discouragement, draw me back to Your presence, where I find clarity, peace, and the strength to press on. With Your guidance and strength, I'll keep moving forward toward the goal, faithfully following You.

Today, I will approach my life with a fresh sense of dedication to my calling, taking every opportunity to grow, serve, and honor Jesus Christ's legacy.

AMEN.

I appeal to you therefore, brothers, by the mercies of God, to present your bodies as a living sacrifice, holy and acceptable to God, which is your spiritual worship. Do not be conformed to this world, but be transformed by the renewal of your mind, that by testing you may discern what is the will of God, what is good and acceptable and perfect. For by the grace given to me I say to everyone among you not to think of himself more highly than he ought to think, but to think with sober judgment, each according to the measure of faith that God has assigned.

— Romans 12:1-3 (ESV)

Responsive Reflections

*Journal about any thoughts or ideas that come to mind in
response to today's prayer and Bible passage.*

_____

_____

_____

_____

_____

_____

_____

_____

_____

_____

_____

_____

God is developing your purpose through your trial, and it's likely that you are currently in process. The process of life cannot come without perseverance.

CORA JAKES COLEMAN

Day 30

DEAR GOD, You give me the power and everything I need to be purposeful. Sometimes my dedication to my goals can become all-consuming, leaving little room for the rest and peace You desire for me. I ask for Your help in finding a balance, in knowing when to diligently work and when to step back and rest in Your provision.

Help me, God, to understand that while my efforts are important, they are not the only means of success. Teach me to leave the results in Your capable hands. I trust that You will guide the outcomes according to Your perfect purpose for Your kingdom.

Grant me the wisdom to recognize the signs of weariness and the humility to admit when I need to pause and replenish. In moments of restlessness and anxiety, remind me that You are the One who grants rest and peace to Your beloved children, like me.

I pray for the discipline to set aside time for rest and reflection, to recharge my body, mind, and spirit. Help me to see rest not as idleness or signs of laziness, but as an essential part of my spiritual and physical well-being.

Sabbath is an act of faith and trust in You. You are in control and my well-being is of utmost importance to You.

Today, I place my plans and efforts into Your hands, trusting that as I rest, You are working my purpose together.

AMEN.

Then Jesus said, "Come to me, all of you who are weary and carry heavy burdens, and I will give you rest. Take my yoke upon you. Let me teach you, because I am humble and gentle at heart, and you will find rest for your souls. For my yoke is easy to bear, and the burden I give you is light."

— Matthew 11:28-30 (NLT)

Responsive Reflections

Journal about any thoughts or ideas that come to mind in response to today's prayer and Bible passage.

Take my
moments and
my days; let
them flow in
ceaseless praise.

FRANCES RIDLEY
HAVERGAL

Day 31

DEAR GOD, So much about my future seems impossible and uncertain. However, I am certain about You and Your desire to lead me in my purpose. I choose to follow You. I am grateful for the opportunity to get to walk with You. Open my ears to hear You and my eyes to see You clearly in all areas of my life.

I don't want to minimize You or put You in a box. Remove any limitations I've placed on our relationship based on unbelief, ignorance, or idolatry. The purpose You have is likely bigger than I could ever think or imagine. Help me to design both my daily and long-term plans in line with Your will, trusting that You know what's best for me.

Give me the courage to move forward, even when I feel unsure or uncomfortable about what's ahead. Teach me how to approach both the familiar and the unknown with unwavering faith. Don't let the words or actions of others, or circumstances beyond my control, make me doubt my worth or calling. I am seen, I am loved, and I am made whole by You. Thank You for loving me so completely.

Today, I will walk in confidence, trusting in Your plan and knowing that I am fully loved and guided by You.

AMEN.

The Spirit of the Sovereign Lord is upon me, for the Lord has anointed me to bring good news to the poor. He has sent me to comfort the brokenhearted and to proclaim that captives will be released and prisoners will be freed...You will be called priests of the Lord, ministers of our God. You will feed on the treasures of the nations and boast in their riches. Instead of shame and dishonor, you will enjoy a double share of honor. You will possess a double portion of prosperity in your land, and ever-lasting joy will be yours. "For I, the Lord, love justice. I hate robbery and wrongdoing. I will faithfully reward my people for their suffering and make an everlasting covenant with them.

— Psalm 61:1,6-8

Responsive Reflections

Journal about any thoughts or ideas that come to mind in response to today's prayer and Bible passage.

_____

_____

_____

_____

_____

_____

_____

_____

_____

_____

_____

_____

_____

It is not on great occasions only that we are required to be faithful to the will of God; occasions constantly occur, and we should be surprised to perceive how much our spiritual advancement depends on small obediences.

ANNIE SOPHIE SWETCHINE

BONUS LESSON: The Power of Prayer

The following are notes from my talk entitled, "The Power of Prayer." This can help you continue dedicating time and focus to prayer as purpose development. You can watch this bonus video lesson immediately here: https://www.learnwithlakeshia.com/powerofprayer. Or you can scan the following QR code with your phone camera to access.

In Mark 9:14-29 (ESV), we witness a powerful story that highlights the vital connection between faith and the effectiveness of prayer. As Jesus and His disciples encounter a father desperate for his son's healing, the narrative unfolds, revealing not only the spiritual battle taking place but also the disciples' struggle. The disciples had previously been successful in casting out demons (Mark 6:7-13), yet in this instance, they failed.

Jesus' response to their inability was not a critique of their technique or words but a rebuke of their lack of faith. There are some theologians who argue that Jesus is speaking to the crowd in general and not his followers, but nevertheless he describes the generation as faithless (Mark 9:19). This highlights a deficiency in belief.

The disciples' struggle in this passage serves as a poignant reminder that the power of prayer is rooted in faith. Jesus emphasized that the kind of miracle needed to heal the boy could only be achieved through prayer (Mark 9:29), which implies a deep, abiding faith and connection with God. Some translations include fasting.

Whether prayer alone or combine with fasting, this spiritual discipline is not about reciting the right words or following a specific formula; it is about a genuine, heartfelt trust in God's power and presence.

A lack of faith will create a disconnect between us and the divine power necessary to perform miracles.

We often quote the model prayer and how Jesus responds to one of his disciples' request to teach them how to pray. However, in this passage if we look a little closer we see a masterclass in the power of prayer.

Before Jesus explains to his followers that "this spirit only comes out through prayer" in verse 29 – which again demonstrates the incredible power of prayer – there is an exchange between Jesus and the man who came to him.

The father's plea, "I believe; help my unbelief!" serves as an example of an honest, vulnerable request of the Lord.

Jesus responds to his sincere desire for greater faith. This teaches us that authentic prayer isn't about perfect or flawless words, but about bringing our whole selves—including our doubts and struggles—before God. The man's cry acknowledges both his faith and his need for more, demonstrating that belief isn't an all-or-nothing proposition but a journey of growth.

Jesus links the power of prayer directly to belief, saying, "All things can be done for the one who believes." Yet, He doesn't dismiss the man for his imperfect faith. Instead, He honors the man's forthright confession of unbelief and responds to his plea, showing us that God meets us where we are, even in our moments of uncertainty.

This passage encourages us to approach God with raw honesty, trusting that He can strengthen our faith even as we struggle with doubt. It reminds us that the very act of crying out to God in our unbelief is itself an act of faith.

The Essence of Prayer

Prayer is often perceived as a means to make requests to God, but it is fundamentally about experiencing His presence. Theologian, philosopher, author and civil rights leader Howard Thurman eloquently stated:

> *"All of us want the assurance of not being deserted by life nor deserted in life. Faith teaches us that God is—that He is the fact of life from which all other things take their meaning and reality. When Jesus prayed, he was conscious that, in his prayer, he met the Presence, and this consciousness was far more important and significant than the answering of his prayer. It is for this reason primarily that God was for Jesus the answer to all the issues and the problems of life. When I, with all my mind and heart, truly seek God and give myself in prayer, I, too, meet His Presence, and then I know for myself that Jesus was right."*

When we pray, we are not just asking for things; we are entering into a divine conversation, seeking to align our hearts with God's will. We are entering into a greater awareness of God's Presence.

Many followers of Jesus Christ can recount personal experiences where prayer has brought about profound changes, providing comfort, guidance, and even miraculous outcomes. These testimonies reinforce the belief that prayer works.

However, there are also times when prayers seem "unanswered," which can challenge our faith.

Prayer is always answered, though not always in the ways we expect or desire. What many perceive as 'unanswered prayer' is often God's response of "no" or "not yet." These answers, while challenging to accept, are integral to our spiritual growth and development. They teach us patience, humility, and trust in God's wisdom and timing. When we encounter these seemingly negative responses, we are presented with an opportunity to deepen our faith and align our will more closely with God's.

Embracing this truth allows us to approach prayer not as a means to bend God's will to ours, but as a way to surrender our will to His, fostering a more mature and resilient faith.

God is God. God is sovereign. We have to get to a point in our faith journey where when things don't "go our way," we relent to the One who is completely in control. Instead of attempting to strong-arm God with spiritual platitudes, learning to navigate tough answers (and even silence) ultimately fortifies your faith.

It is in these moments that our belief is tested. The persistence in prayer demonstrates a deeper level of trust in who God is, even when we do not fully understand His ways. Hebrews 11:6 states:

> *And without faith it is impossible to please him, for whoever would approach God must believe that he exists and that he rewards those who seek him.*

This passage underscores that the act of praying itself is a testament to our belief in God's existence and His responsiveness to our earnest seeking.

The truth is, faith is less about coming up with some step-by-step formulaic prayer and more about allowing ourselves to be perfected through the process of prayer and presence of God.

God isn't looking for polished words or a specific technique. He's looking for sincere hearts that are open to His guidance.

I remember a time when I felt lost in my prayer life. I didn't know how to pray "correctly," and it created a distance between God and me. But then I did something simple yet profound – I asked God to teach me how to pray. And you know what? He answered. He prompted me to start praying for others, and through that, my prayer life transformed.

This experience taught me that God is more than willing to guide us in our prayer journey. He wants to communicate with us, and He understands our struggles. If you're feeling unsure about how to pray, take heart. Turn that uncertainty into a prayer itself. Ask God to teach you, to guide you, to show you how to connect with Him.

Remember, prayer is a relationship, not a performance. It's about opening your heart to God, not reciting perfect words. As you continue to pray, even when you feel unsure, you'll find that God will meet you where you are. He will teach you, grow you, and deepen your connection with Him. This journey of learning to pray is itself a beautiful form of prayer and a powerful way to grow in your faith.

A thriving prayer life is a reflection of a vibrant faith, one that trusts in God's goodness and dominion. Therefore, cultivating a habit of prayer is essential for nurturing and demonstrating our belief in God.

Want more? Click/tap on the image to watch the talk based on these notes on Lakeshia Poole's YouTube Channel: https://www.learnwithlakeshia.com/powerofprayer

About the Author

Lakeshia Poole is a passionate storyteller, speaker, and author of eight titles, including *Purposeful Prayers, Faith Beats Fear, Renew: 40 Prayers and Prompts to Power Up Your Life,* and *Happily Ever Christmas.* From the screen to the stage, she inspires individuals to elevate their lives through the power of words. She currently serves on the speaking team at Legacy Church.